ATTENTION BOOK WRITER:

This book is a template for you to use to complete the book. provided the font type, size and style, along with the format. also provided the introduction, conclusion and additional sections of the book. For this project research and fill out the Chapters of this book with the number of words requested in the project details. Feel free to change the numbers of chapters and provide names for each chapter as you wish.

Please Fill in the introduction and write a conclusion. Make sure the introduction is at least 1 page long.

Please write a 200-300 word description that sells the book. Please put that after the conclusion for me. Thank You.

This book should be about how to make herbal soap from scratch. Please make this book very detailed and include specifics. Below I have a list of different things that should be included in the book please make sure to include each one.

- Herbal Soap 101
- Natural & Herbal Ingredients
- Its Powerful Benefits
- Recipes for (Relaxation, Skin, Antiseptic & Healing)

Herbal Soap Making:

A Simple guide to making Herbal Soaps that Cleanse the Pours and Nurtures the Body

Table Of Contents

Introduction

I want to thank you and congratulate you for downloading the book "Herbal Soap Making: A Simple Guide to Making Herbal Soaps that Cleanse the Pores and Nurtures the Body."

This book contains proven steps and strategies on how to become a truly accomplished herbal soap maker.

Here's an inescapable fact: you will need to be inventive, creative, and innovative if you would like to be ahead. Soap making allows all of these qualities to flourish. Not only that, the benefits to be reaped are truly remarkable. Making herbal soaps can start out as a hobby but it can eventually be a delightful lifetime staple. Making herbal soaps is good for the body and good for the environment as well.

If you do not develop your soap making skills as soon as you can, then you will be missing out on a wonderful opportunity.

It's time for you to become an amazing home maker of amazing herbal soaps that will surely help you cleanse your skin's pores and nurture the rest of your body.

Chapter 1: Herbal Soap 101

What is Soap?

Soap is an item that is generally used with water for cleaning and washing. It is a compound of oils or fats and an alkaline substance such as sodium hydroxide or lye.

What are Herbs?

Herbs are plants with leaves, flowers, and seeds that are generally used for food, flavoring, medicine, and perfume.

What is an Herbal Soap?

Herbal soaps are usually homemade or handmade soaps with herbs incorporated into the mixture.

The Powerful Benefits of Herbal Soaps:

1. With all-natural ingredients, herbal soaps cause less inflammation and allergic reactions on the skin.

2. Herbal soaps have properties beyond cleaning. They benefit the skin, promote relaxation, and help heal the body as well

3. Herbal soaps can be used every day for long periods of time without blocking pores and causing side effects.

4. They do not dry out the skin and have moisturizing properties that keep it well-hydrated.

5. The natural ingredients make it environment-friendly as there is nothing that can potentially cause damage when it decomposes or "goes back" to the earth.

6. You can control exactly how much or how little of the ingredients you want to use. The ingredients can be according to what you have on hand or what is easily accessible or available.

Definition of Soap Making Terms

1. **Tracing:** This is the sign that the chemical process of soap making is going smoothly. This is seen when some of the soap mixture is taken up and allowed to drip back. A trace is seen when the dribbled soap makes a mark on the surface of the soap mixture. Other clues of tracing include: opacity, thickening, and wafting up of soap smells.

2. **Saponification:** This term literally means "to turn into soap." This is the reaction of the lye and the oils used in soap making.

3. **Super-fatting:** This term, otherwise known as lye discount, refers to the process of using less lye and more oils or fats in the soap making process. This makes the soap gentler on the skin and softer to the touch. Another way of super-fatting is to add extra oils to the soap batter before pouring into a mold.

Chapter 2: Herbal Soap Making Tools and Equipment

Safety Equipment

1. **Eye Protection:** They should be resistant top caustic chemicals, force or impact, and heat

2. **Gloves:** These are to protect your hands and arms without hindering finger movement. Textured fingers are helpful for a good grip of other tools and equipments. Examples: Rubber kitchen gloves and examination gloves.

3. **Face Masks:** These are for protection from caustic steam. Examples: filter mask or painter's paper dust mask.

4. **Fire Extinguisher**

5. **Vinegar:** This acts as a neutralizer in case of contact with lye and raw soap mixtures. It is an acid that works against the alkaline properties of the soap ingredients.

Measuring Tools and Equipment

1. **Scale:** The main way of measuring the specific ingredients for soap making is by weight. The most important point to remember is accuracy.

   o Features to look out for:

      ✓ The scale is able to automatically reset to zero when adding ingredients

      ✓ Scales that are able to measure both in grams and ounces

      ✓ Scales that can measure in tenths of ounces

      ✓ Digital scales- these are optional but most soap makers prefer this as it is more accurate and has multiple features.

2. **Measuring Cups and Spoons:** Stainless steel and glass are the best ones to use for soap making.

3. **Droppers:** This is specifically for recipes that call for drops of essential oils or fragrances.

4. **Thermometers:** For accurate measurements of temperature throughout the soap making process.

Pots and Pans

The ideal pots and pans are made of stainless steel as other kinds of pots such as aluminum, tin, cast iron, and nonstick varieties can cause a reaction with the ingredients of the soap. Enameled pots and pans can be used but they should always be checked for pits or chips that can possibly expose the soap mixture to the reactive metals underneath.

1. **Stock Pot:** One helpful feature to look out for are those with gradient markings for volume.

2. **Double Boiler**

3. **Slow Cooker:** The size requirements should be just right for the batch of soap to be made. If it is too small or too big, the soap mixture will not process properly.

Stainless Steel Utensils: All sorts of stainless utensils may be used throughout the soap making process. The most common are spoons for stirring and mashers for breaking down big solid pieces of ingredients. Make sure that the connectors such as screws and bolts are made of stainless steel as well to prevent any reactions with other metals.

Silicone Utensils: The most commonly used of this variety are spatulas or scrapers. It is best to use a one-piece type of model to prevent loss of any utensil part especially when making big batches of soap.

Wooden Utensils: Wooden spoons, especially the long-handled ones, can be used to stir soap mixtures or batters. Make sure that the utensils are free from splinters and are sturdy enough to stir through thick mixtures. It is important to remember that lye-based soaps may eventually eat through the wooden material of the utensils. Other possible wooden utensils that may be helpful are chopsticks and wooden skewers.

Hand Blender or Immersion Blender: This is optional but it makes stirring a lot faster and easier. The best ones to use have a plastic housing and stainless steel blades. The shaft should ideally be long enough to reach the bottom of the pot or pan being used.

Soap Molds:

- ✓ **Home-made Molds:** These can be made out of cardboard lined with wax paper for easy unmolding.

- ✓ **Commercial Soap Molds:** There are soap molds that are available for purchase but alternatives to this include: cookie cutter molds, cupcake trays, and ice cube trays.

- ✓ **Polymer Clay Molds:** These allow the soap maker to make impressions or designs on the soap. The downside is that the resulting soaps tend to become brittle.

- ✓ **Box molds:** These can either be purchased or hand-made. They are basically wooden boxes specifically made to hold soap mixtures until they harden sufficiently.

- ✓ **Creative molds:** Anything of interest may be used such as big sea shells, old toys, embossed bowls, little shot glasses, carved bowls, etc.

Cutting Tools:

- ✓ Kitchen Knives: The best knives are stainless steel and non serrated for a clean and even cut.

- ✓ Putty knives

- ✓ Cheese cutters

- ✓ Dough scrapers

Chapter 3: The Basic Herbal Soap Ingredients

The three ingredients that are needed to make soap are: lye, a liquid to dissolve the lye, and oils or fats. All the others are extras and considered as additives to enhance the basic properties of the soap.

Lye or Sodium Hydroxide: This is the alkaline base of the soap that reacts with the acidic ingredients to bring out the needed properties of the soap.

Water: This ingredient is used to firstly activate the lye and secondly disperse the oils used in the mixture. It evaporates during the curing process that the soap eventually undergoes. The choices range from seawater, rainwater, well water, distilled water, and scented water. Milk can be used as a replacement as well if desired.

Other Liquids that Can be Used:

- Coffee

- Tea

- Herb infusions

- Beer

- Fruit juices

Oils and Fats: These are the acidic components of the soap that react with the lye. They are often chosen according to their properties that make the soap hard and/ or easy to lather.

> **Note:** Super-fats are the extra oils that are added during the end of the soap making process that are meant to be free-floating and not combined with the lye. This makes the soap more moisturizing.

- **Animal Fats or Oils:** These are in the form of tallow and lard or beef and pork fat respectively. They are first rendered before used in the soap making process.

- **Beeswax**: This ingredient adds fragrance and hardness to the soap. It is recommended to use only small amounts as it tends to stop lathering when used in large quantities.

- **Cocoa Butter**: Thus ingredient provides moisture, hydration, and skin protection. It also helps to harden the soap.

- **Coconut Oil**: This ingredient hardens the soap and provides lather and cleansing properties as well. It is moisturizing and has anti-inflammatory properties.

- **Olive Oil:** This ingredient is used for sensitive skin but is also compatible with other skin types. This ingredient hardens the soap bar and provides a barrier for the skin that keeps moisture in.

- **Hempseed Oil:** This oil is rich in anti-oxidants. It has anti-aging, healing, and protective properties.

- **Soybean Oil:** This ingredient is used for its conditioning properties and ability to create a stable lather

- **Shea Butter:** This is most often used as a super fat and has moisturizing and hydrating properties. It can help to reverse skin damage.

- **Sweet Almond Oil**: This is a super-fatting oil that is used for its light feeling. It has the ability to moisturize and condition the skin.

Antioxidants: These are ingredients that keep the super-fatting oils of the soap from going rancid. They keep the free-floating oils stable and preserved.

- **Grapefruit Seed Extract:** This is from the seeds and pulp of grapefruits. It is a thick, clear, and scentless liquid that keeps the oils from spoiling.

- **Rosemary Oleoresin Extract:** This ingredient is extracted from the leaves of the rosemary plant. It has a strong smelling quality to it.

Optional Ingredients

1. Fragrance: Essential oils are the natural choice while fragrance oils are the commercially-produced ones. Depending on your taste and preference, either one can be used.

- **Essential Oil:** These healing and medical properties aside from smelling good. The downsides are that they are usually expensive and tend to fade overtime especially when the soap is exposed to sunlight.

- **Fragrance Oils:** They are generally inexpensive and have more selection for scents that last longer. The downside is not knowing the exact ingredients. Most contain petrochemicals and allergens that can cause anaphylactic reactions for sensitive people.

2. Scent Fixer: These are ingredients that are used to make the fragrance of the soap last longer. Examples of natural scent fixers are:

- Arrowroot

- Cornstarch

- Oatmeal

- Essential oils like cedarwood and patchouli

3. Soap Coloring

- **Oils:** Olive oil will make the soap have a yellowish or creamy color while light colored oils yield to a white colored soap.

- **Coffee, tea, and milk:** Using these liquids to dissolve the lye can result in brownish or caramel colored soaps.

- **Clays:** They make the soap pink or red, green, and/ or white.

    o Rose Clay gives a color ranging from light pink to brick red

    o Sea clay give a grayish green color to the soap

- o Bentonite clay gives a light green or a greenish grey color as well.

- **Minerals and Mica Powder:** They generally can make the soap in any desired color.

- **Sugars:** Any added sugar, honey, and/ or milk to the soap will caramelize and provide a yellowish or brownish tint.

- **Herbs, Flowers, and Plant Roots:** Depending on the specific ingredient added, they provide color as well as texture to the soap. Examples:

  - o calendula petals make the soap orange

  - o madder root provides a pink color

  - o spearmint makes the soap pale yellow

  - o peppermint makes the soap yellow-green

  - o Lemon balm gives the soap a creamy yellow color

  - o Comfrey leaves makes the herbal soap green while the comfrey roots yields a brown color

  - o Finely ground basil makes the soap green as well

  - o Cinnamon and elderberry make the soap brown

  - o Mace powder make the soap orange

  - o Annatto seed makes yellow soap

  - o Beet root makes the soap red or pink depending on how much of the herb infusion is used.

4. **Others:** Dried fruits, spices, flowers, leaves, and plant roots can be added to the soap to provide fragrance, decoration, color, visual interest, texture and exfoliation to the herbal soap.

  - **Honey:** It has healing and moisturizing properties that are good for the skin in general. A good amount to start with is one tablespoon for every pound of oils.

- **Glycerin:** This is a moisturizing agent that is added to lye based soaps. One tablespoon of glycerin is enough for every pound of oil.

- **Silk:** These are proteins that can be added to the soap. Liquefied silk, silk fibers silk powders, and silk fabric can be added to the lye solution to make the resulting soap feel smoother.

- **Grains and Seeds:** These can be added for exfoliation and as visual interests. Examples of commonly used ingredients in soaps include: cornmeal, oatmeal, poppy seeds, coffee, and berry seeds.

- **Other exfoliating agents:** crushed pumice stone, bamboo powder, and vanilla bean powder.

- **Cosmetic clays:** They can be used not only for their coloring properties but also for their oil-absorbing properties as well.

Chapter 4: The Soap Making Process

Using Animal Fat for Soap Making

Step One: Rendering the Fat

1. Prepare the Ingredients: one pound of beef fat, one and a half of pork fat, and water
2. Melt each animal fat in separate pots or pans on low heat.
3. When fully melted, strain the liquefied fat through a strainer lined with paper towels. This is to remove any solid food particles called cracklings.
4. Add equal parts of warm water to each liquefied fat still in separate pots or pans.
5. Bring both mixtures to a boil and then simmer for fifteen minutes.
6. Pour one quart of cold water in each pot, stir, and cool overnight in a refrigerator.
7. Lift out the hardened animal fat on the next day and remove the remaining water.
8. Pat off any excess water and store in the freezer.

Step Two: Making the Soap

1. Gather the needed ingredients.

   - One and one third cups of melted tallow or beef fat
   - Two and two thirds cup of melted lard or pork fat
   - One and one fourth cups of cold water
   - One half cup and one and a half teaspoons of lye
   - Additives like essential oils

2. Prepare the molds and line them with paper as necessary.
3. Make a lye solution by carefully pouring the lye on the water.

   Note: the solution will start to steam and heat up

4. Allow the lye solution to cool down to room temperature.

5. When properly cooled, stir in the lye solution to the combined tallow and lard. They should all be at room temperature.

6. Stir or blend the mixture until it thickens and tracing happens. This is the time to put in the additives or scented oils. Blend thoroughly before pouring into ready molds. Store in a cool and dry area.

7. Wait for twenty four hours before unmolding the soap and cutting.

8. Place the cut soap into appropriate containers and cure for at least three weeks before using.

Using Vegetable Fat for Soap Making

The Cold Process Technique: There is basically no heating used in this technique aside from liquefying solid oils. The preferred blend of oils is mixed with a solution of lye and water. The new mixture is then stirred or blended until it thickens and poured into a ready mold.

Advantages:

- The soap are made in large batches
- The cooking time is relatively low
- The resulting soap bars are long lasting

Disadvantages:

- The ingredients should be measured as accurately as possible or else the soap will fail.
- The curing time is very long
- The resulting soap mixture is not so easily molded

The Process:

Step One: Prepare your work area.

- Work in a place away from children and pets
- Work in a well-ventilated and well-lighted area with easy access to a water source or a working faucet.

Step Two: Prepare the tools and equipment.

- Line the soap molds with freezer paper or wax paper as necessary
- Spray the insides of plastic trays with an oil-based non-stick spray

Step Three: Put on the required safety equipment.

- It is best to keep all of the safety gear on until after all the soap making equipments are cleaned.

Step Four: Weigh all needed ingredients.

- Weigh the solid oils
- Weigh the liquid oils
- Weigh the super-fat oils
- Weigh the selected additives such as essential oils or botanicals
- Weigh the water needed for the batch of soap
- Weigh the lye crystals needed

Step Five: Create an ice bath by filling the sink or a container with ice and water.

Step Six: Slightly heat all the solid oils until they are completely melted. Remove from heat before adding the liquid oils.

Step Seven: Place the previously weighed water in a heat-proof container and on to the ice bath. Slowly add in the lye to the water. This step produces steam as the lye reacts with the water. Stir the lye carefully until it is approximately thirty five degrees Celsius.

Step Eight: Stir the oil mixture until it reaches twenty six degrees Celsius. Stir the lye and water solution separately until it reaches the same temperature.

Step Nine: When both the mixtures have reached the right temperatures, carefully pour the lye solution into the oil mixture. Stir until both are smoothly incorporated. An immersion blender may be used after the initial stirring to speed up the process.

Note: By hand, the stirring may take up to fifteen minutes to an hour; with a hand blender it takes five to ten minutes.

Step Ten: Add in the super-fats, essential oils, and botanicals, and other additives. Blend or stir until the batter gets thicker and hardens a bit- this is called tracing.

Step Eleven: Pour the mixture into previously prepared molds and cover. Place in a warm area and let the molded mixtures sit for twenty four hours.

Step Twelve: Uncover the soap and let it sit for another twenty four hours.

Step Thirteen: Unmold the soap and cure or air dry for about four to six weeks.

The Hot Process Technique: This technique is an extension of the cold process method. Instead of pouring the soap batter into a mold after mixing, it is heated and cooked for a few hours until it neutralizes. The soap does not need to be cured; it can be used right away.

> **Note:** Neutrality is measured with litmus paper or phenolphthalein. Put a few drops of phenolphthalein on the soap and if the drops remain clear, the soap is already neutral. If the drops turn pink, the soap is alkaline and needs to cook longer.

Advantages:

- The artistic options are almost endless

- There curing time is faster than that of the cold process technique.

Disadvantages:

- The soap mixture tends to harden quickly as they are poured into the molds

- They are not easy to mold

- The soaps require more fragrance elements as the high cooking temperatures burn off the scent.

Making Herbal Soaps without Handling Lye

If there is some concern about handling lye as it is caustic and potentially dangerous, several other methods of soap making can be employed. These methods still have lye content but are in a form of base soaps that are safer to handle. This means that the lye crystals are not used directly in the soap making processes.

The Soap-Casting Technique: This is otherwise known as the melt-and-pour technique that most often uses a glycerin soap base. The glycerin soap can be either handmade or purchased as a whole. The glycerin soap is chopped and melted in a pot to allow the mixture of essential oils, botanicals, and other additive ingredients.

Advantages:

- The artistic options are almost endless

- It is very easy to do

- The process is very versatile

- This process is safe to do with children.

- There is no curing needed, the soaps can be used after they are cool enough to unmold.

Disadvantages:

- The soaps do not last as long as those made through the cold process technique

- The soaps do not lather as well as those made through the cold process technique

- There is less control over the ingredients as the base soap is already made.

- The purchased base soaps can be expensive.

Commonly Used Base Soaps:

- Hemp Glycerin Soap

- Olive Oil Soaps

- Clear Glycerin Soap

- Goat's Milk Glycerin Soap

The Hand Milling Technique: Any type of soap, hot processed or cold processed, is grated, heated, and mixed in with various additives to make a completely new soap. It is placed into molds and allowed to set.

Making Liquid Soaps

Step One: Make a regular solid soap according to the normal instructions excepting the one about curing time.

Step Two: After unmolding the soap, make it into smaller pieces: cut, shave, chop, or shred according to preference.

Step Three: Place chopped soap and water at a ratio of one cup to three, in a double boiler on medium heat. Stir the mixture until it is fully melted and combined.

Note: The mixture should be extremely runny. Add more water if necessary.

Step Four: Add four tablespoons of vegetable-based glycerin and half a teaspoon of grapefruit seed extract (this is for a cup of soap and three cups water; adjust as necessary for bigger batches.) Essential oils can be added at six to ten drops for every five hundred milliliters of soap. The shelf life of the liquid soap is approximately six to eight months.

Ways of Adding Herbs to Soaps

Direct Addition of Herbs: The easiest and most obvious way of adding herbs to soaps is to sprinkle them while the soap batter or mixture is being poured into a mold. It is best to use dried herbs when doing this. The water in fresh herbs may cause the soap to develop molds later on.

Herb Infusions: Herbs can be infused either in water or oil. This is done by allowing the herbs to steep in hot water or oil. This infusion is then combined with oils and lye to make the soap. Another option is to add ground herbs to the hot water as lye is being poured in. Olive oil is the most common choice for oil infusions of herbs.

Herbal Powders: The dried herbs can be pulverized and powdered for easy addition to the soap mixture while heating or before being put into the mold.

Herbs and soap making techniques

- Soap Casting: Herbs can be added in the bottom, middle or top of the bar by controlling the temperatures of the soap process.

- Hand Milling: Shredded herbs can be added to the grated soap before re-melting. This process retrains most of the herb's properties.

- Hot Process Technique: The herbs are added right before the soap mixture is placed into the molds.

Chapter 5: Soap Making Tips, Tricks, and Advice

Safety Measures:

- Never add water to lye crystals. This could be a cause for an explosion. Always pour the lye into water and not vice versa.

- Work in a well-ventilated area to avoid excessive inhalation of fumes.

- Prepare and measure all ingredients accurately before mixing.

First Aid for Lye and Raw Soap Spills:

Vinegar can be used as a neutralizer for lye in cases of spills. It is a weak acid that will neutralize the alkaline properties of the lye in the soap mixture.

1. Blot the soap mixture with an absorbent material off the skin.

2. Flush the affected area with running water.

3. Douse the affected area with vinegar.

4. Flush the area again with running water.

5. Wash the area with soap and water.

6. Seek medical attention as necessary.

Making an Improvised Double Boiler:

Use a wide-mouthed pot or sauce pan and a slightly smaller stainless bowl that fits securely bit nit tightly on the pot or pan. Fill the pot with water and use the stainless bowl to melt or heat the needed ingredients.

Troubleshooting Tips:

- Soap mixtures that are too hot can warp molds especially if they are made of plastic

- Soaps that are difficult to unmold may not be cooled enough. Put the soap mold into the freezer for about ten minutes before unmolding again.

- The best time to add scents and fragrances is when the soap mixture has cooled to about fifty one degrees Celsius. This is just before the soap mixture is poured into their molds.

- Avoid food coloring to dye soaps as they can stain the skin when the soap is used later.

Common Soap Making Problems:

1. There is no tracing in the soap batter or mixture

Causes:

- Incorrect solution temperatures
- Stirring or blending too slowly
- Putting in too much water

Solutions:

- Measure the correct amount of water as accurately as possible
- Make sure all of the oils and lye are added to the mixture.
- Stir the mixture consistently with a hand blender if possible

2. The soap batter or mixture begins to form streaks

Causes: The mixture is too cold

Solutions:

- Make sure the temperatures of the ingredients are adequate for each step.
- If more signs of tracing are noted, pour the mixtures into the mold.

3. The soap batter or mixture begins to curdle

Cause: This is common when synthetic fragrance oils are used

4. The soap batter or mixture has solid chunks of ingredients

Causes:

- The oil or lye solutions were too hot when poured
- The stirring or blending is too slow and/ or inconsistent

5. The soap batter or mixture becomes grainy

Causes:

- The mixture is too hot or too cold
- The stirring or blending is too slow and/ or inconsistent

6. The soap is brittle; it cracks and/or breaks when being unmolded or cut

Causes:

- There are too much dry ingredients.
- The tracing stage was too long

7. The soap has a thin white layer on the surface

Cause: This is a natural reaction of the soap mixture to air.

8. The soap has chunks of solid lye but the rest of the soap is soft and the bottom has a slippery liquid layer.

Causes:

- The mixture was poured into the mold too soon
- The stirring or blending is too slow and/ or inconsistent

Note: These soap bars may irritate the skin if used.

9. The soap has air bubbles

Cause: This is common when the soap batter is stirred too fast and too long.

10. **The soap has a lot of whitish powder on the top layer; it is cakey and crumbly**

Causes:

- Hard water may have been used in the mixture

Note: These soap bars may irritate the skin if used. Make sure to use distilled water for the next batches of soap.

Tips for Finishing Homemade Herbal Soaps

- Smoothen the soap surface by buffing with an abrasive cloth or a piece of wool
- Use a knife to pare off a thin layer from the soap surface
- Personalize the soaps with embossed molds
- Wrap the soap in pieces of cloth and twine

Creating Your Own Herbal Soap Recipe

Step One: Choose the best soap making method for you.
- Take note of the availability of ingredients
- Canvass for the materials, tools, and supplies needed
- Note the easiest and most comfortable for you to do according to your soap making skill level

Step Two: Determine what kind of soap you want to make. Some Suggestions:
- Decorative soaps
- Moisturizing soaps
- Aromatherapy soaps
- Exfoliating soap bars
- Soaps for treating acne and other blemishes
- Whitening soaps
- Fun soaps for children

Step Three: Choosing the details and elements to be incorporated into the soap

- Are you going to super-fat?
- What colors would you want the soaps to be?
- Do you want the soap to be unscented or fragrant?
- What are the additives you plan to add?
    - Dried flowers
    - Essential oils
    - Clays

Step Four: Experiment and make notes of special points for future reference

Step Five: Putting finishing touches
- The shape of the soap
- The texture, whether rough or smooth
- The packaging
- Embossed or carved designs

Chapter 6: List of Natural and Herbal Ingredients

1. **Aloe Vera:** Provides moisture and is used to heal minor burns. It has antifungal properties as well.

2. **Alfalfa:** This is used to relieve signs of fatigue, muscle soreness and tenderness, and pain from arthritis and rheumatism.

3. **Arnica Flower:** This herb has wound-healing capabilities.

4. **Barberry:** It is an antifungal agent that is useful for skin infections.

5. **Basil:** This herb has antibacterial properties and is used to treat skin rashes and minor skin irritations.

6. **Beer Hops:** It has relaxing properties that soothe irritated skin and antibacterial properties as well.

7. **Bentonite Clay:** Although not an herb, this can be used in soaps for its qualities of removing toxins in the body.

8. **Borage:** This herb has anti-inflammatory and emollient properties that make the skin moisturized and well-hydrated.

9. **Broad Leaf Plantain:** This is a natural wound healing plant that helps to staunch blood flow. It has both antibacterial and anti-inflammatory properties.

10. **Calendula:** This herb had multiple uses. It can soothe inflammations, sprains, rashes, and irritated skin. It can also help to reduce the appearance of scars.

11. **Chamomile:** This herb has soothing and calming abilities. Its anti-inflammatory and antibacterial properties help in wound healing. It is used to treat: acne, skin irritations, bruises, and diaper rash.

12. **Cardamom**: This herb has properties that can improve the body's blood circulation. It is energizing, uplifting, and gives off a feeling of warmth.

13. **Cinnamon:** This ingredient helps to reduce stress. It is used as an astringent and a stimulant as well.

14. **Cloves:** This is uplifting and mentally stimulating although it can be irritating for people with sensitive skin.

15. **Coffee:** Coffee grounds mixed in soap can help to exfoliate the skin. It also helps to treat acne, smoothen the skin, and acts as a deodorizer.

16. **Dandelion:** This plant has healing properties and as well as being an astringent.

17. **Eucalyptus:** It has a soothing and calming effect that is helpful for fevers, headaches, muscular pain, and respiratory problems. It has antibacterial and insect repellent properties as well.

18. **Forsythia:** This plant has edible flowers and has antiviral properties.

19. **Green tea:** This is naturally rich in antioxidants, flavonoids, and indoles that help boost the body's immune system.

20. **Lavender:** This natural ingredient has properties that are soothing, calming, cleansing, and healing.

21. **Lemongrass:** It can help to keep the skin from being oily. It has a relaxing and sedative effect and is used to treat headaches.

22. **Licorice Root:** It is an anti-inflammatory and an emollient. It can also help to reduce and prevent hyper-pigmentation of the skin.

23. **Marshmallow Root:** This herb has properties that are soothing, lubricating, softening, and healing. It is also able to relieve mild pain.

24. **Mint:** It is fragrant and has cooling and soothing properties. It can boost one's mood as well.

25. **Nasturtium:** This plant has an astringent effect.

26. **Neem:** Extracts from this plant are antiseptic and antibacterial which helps to prevent skin disorders.

27. **Oatmeal:** This acts as an emollient for dry skin and as an oil absorber for oily skin. It is also a natural exfoliant that is usable for those with sensitive skin. It has anti-inflammatory properties that helps to relieve insect bites and discomfort from too much sun exposure.

28. **Papaya:** This has whitening properties that help to make the skin tone look more even.

29. **Peppermint:** This plant is known for its cooling capabilities. It is also useful in treating rashes and insect bites.

30. **Rose:** It helps to reduce redness on the skin due to its tonic and astringent properties. It is good for all skin types.

31. **Rosemary:** It is a stimulant with some anti-inflammatory properties.

32. **Sandalwood:** This ingredient has a calming effect. It also helps in the process of removing blemishes.

33. **Tea Tree:** This is used to treat acne and skin rashes and is also known for being soothing. It has antiseptic, antibacterial, and deodorizing properties as well.

34. **Turmeric:** Its antiseptic properties help to prevent skin rashes and skin infections. It also helps to improve the complexion and make the surface of the skin smooth.

35. **Yarrow:** This plant has mild analgesic properties that help to reduce pain. It is also used to treat the swelling caused by burns and abrasions.

36. **Ylang Ylang:** Its uses in aromatherapy include soothing feelings of anger and frustration.

37. **Wheat germ:** This ingredient is used for exfoliation. It also has properties that soften and soothe the skin.

Chapter 7: Herbal Soap Recipes

<u>**Base Soap Recipes:**</u>

1. How to Make Glycerin with a Basic Soap Recipe

Ingredients:
- Two tablespoons of lye
- One cup of water
- One cup of coconut oil
- One cup of olive oil
- One half cup salt

Instructions:

1. Make a lye solution by pouring the lye on the water.

2. Combine the oils together thoroughly and put on high heat before adding the lye solution. Maintain a temperature of fifty one degrees Celsius until the mixture is thoroughly blended then reduce the temperature to thirty seven degrees Celsius.

3. Once the soap batter has thickened and tracing occurs, add in the salt and allow the mixture to cool. Upon cooling, the soap mixture will be seen curdling on top and the glycerin is left under it.

4. Skim off the soap batter from the top of the mixture, pour into molds, and cure.

5. Pour the liquid glycerin into a glass bottle. Seal the bottle tightly and store in the refrigerator.

Note: The glycerin has a shelf life of about three to four weeks.

2. Basic Unscented Soap

Ingredients:
- Three fourths cup of lye
- One and one third cups of distilled water

- One and a half cups of liquefied coconut oil
- Two cups of palm oil
- Two and a half cups of olive oil

Instructions:

1. Make a lye solution by pouring the lye on the distilled water.
2. Combine the oils together thoroughly before adding to the lye solution. Stir until it thickens and tracing happens.
3. Pour into molds, allow to cool, and cure

3. Clear Glycerin Soap

Ingredients:

- Oils: either castor, almond, palm, coconut, avocado, or canola
- Ninety seven percent alcohol at thirty five percent the amount of oils to be used
- Lye at one percent the amount of oils to used
- Water at least 1.2 times the amount of lye to be used
- Glycerin at fifteen percent of the amount of oils to be used
- Two and a half cups of olive oil
- Dissolved sugar at twenty eight percent the amount of oils to be used

Instructions:

1. Put a glass in the refrigerator to be used later in the procedure for soap testing.
2. Make a lye solution by pouring the lye on the water.
3. Combine the oils together thoroughly before adding to the lye solution.
4. Stir the solution until it thickens in consistency and slowly turns into soap.

5. Remove from the source of heat and fold in half the amount of the alcohol and all of the glycerin. Too much stirring will cause the alcohol to evaporate.

6. Cover the pot tightly with its lid and put a towel over it to prevent leakage of the alcohol.

7. Put the pot containing the mixture over another pot with water- basically create an improvised double boiler.

8. Put the double boiler on low heat then uncover the pot and stir on and off for three minutes at a time. Keep the pot covered when not stirring.

9. Ten minutes in to the stirring, add in the rest of the alcohol. The intermittent three minute stirring is done for about fifteen to thirty minutes until the solidified or thickened soap mixture is completely dissolved in the alcohol.

10. When completely dissolved, allow the soap mixture to sit in the double boiler for fifteen minutes.

11. Add in the dissolved sugar and gently stir.

12. Get out the chilled glass and place a few drops of the soap mixture on it. The soap will turn solid almost immediately and show you whether it turns out clear or cloudy.

13. If the mixture is cloudy, cook it some more with alcohol or glycerin. Another option is to let it cool down and firm up to be cooked again on the next day for ten to fifteen minutes without any additional ingredients.

14. If it turns out clear, pour the mixture into the molds and allow it to cool down before unmolding, cutting, and curing.

4. Goat's Milk Soap:

Ingredients:
- Three fourths cup of lye
- One and one third cups of goat's milk
- One and a half cups of liquefied coconut oil
- Two cups of palm oil
- Two and a half cups of olive oil

Instructions:

1. Pour the lye over the goat's milk to make a lye solution.

2. Combine the oils together thoroughly before adding to the lye solution.

3. Stir until tracing is noticed

4. Pour into molds, allow to cool, and cure

Herbal Soap Recipes for Relaxation

1. Lavender Herbal Soap

Ingredients:

- Three fourths cup of lye
- One and one third cups of distilled water
- One and a half cups of liquefied coconut oil
- Two cups of palm oil
- Two and a half cups of olive oil
- One half cup of dried lavender flowers
- A few drops of lavender essential oil

Instructions:

1. Make a lye solution by pouring the lye on the distilled water.

2. Combine the oils together thoroughly before adding to the lye solution.

3. When signs of tracing are noted or when the soap batter has thickened, stir in the dried lavender flowers.

4. Pour into molds, allow to cool, and cure

2. Chamomile Herbal Soap

Ingredients:

- One eighth cup of aloe vera oil

- One cup of coconut oil
- One third cup of palm oil
- One cup of shea butter
- One and a half cups of chamomile tea
- A handful of dried chamomile flowers (optional)
- One half olive oil
- Half a cup of lye

Instructions:

1. Make a lye solution by pouring the lye on the chamomile tea.
2. Combine the oils and fats together thoroughly before adding to the lye solution.
3. When signs of tracing are noted or when the soap batter has thickened, stir in the dried chamomile flowers.
4. Pour into molds, allow to cool, and set before cutting.

Herbal Soaps for Blemish-Prone Skin

1. Lavender and Rosemary Soap

Ingredients:

- Three cups of a glycerin soap base
- One fourth cup of a lavender and rosemary infusion:
  - One cup hot water
  - Three tablespoons lavender leaves and rosemary leaves
- One and a half teaspoons of lavender oil

Instructions:

1. Make the infusion by pouring hot water on the lavender flowers and rosemary leaves and letting it steep for about ten minutes.

2. Combine the melted glycerin base with the herbal infusion. Stir until well-blended and pour into ready molds after the stage of tracing.

3. Cool the mixture and allow to set before cutting.

2. Ylang Ylang and Frankincense Soap

Ingredients:
- Two cups of powdered frankincense
- One eighth cup liquid glycerin
- One eighth cup of aloe vera gel
- One teaspoon ylang ylang essential oil

Instructions:
1. Mix the powdered frankincense with the liquid glycerin.
2. Combine the melted glycerin soap base with the rest of the herbal ingredients and stir until the mixture traces.
3. Pour into the molds before cooling and cutting.

Herbal Soaps for Dry Skin

1. Aloe Vera and Nettle Soap

Ingredients:
- One cup of a glycerin soap base
- One eighth cup of aloe vera gel
- Two teaspoons of crushed nettle leaves

Instructions:
1. Melt the glycerin soap base and combine with the other ingredients.
2. Stir until the mixture has signs of tracing
3. Pour into available molds and cool before cutting.

2. Avocado Soap

Ingredients:
- One half cup and one and a half teaspoons of avocado oil
- One half cup and one teaspoon of palm oil
- One half cup of palm kernel oil
- Seven teaspoons of sweet almond oil
- Four and a half tablespoons of lye
- Six tablespoons of avocado puree
- Six tablespoons of water

Instructions:
1. Make a lye solution by adding the lye to half of the specified amount of water.
2. Heat the oils and blend well before adding the rest of the water with the avocado puree and the lye solution.
3. Stir until the mixture has signs of tracing
4. Pour into available molds and cool before cutting.

3. Brown Sugar, Fig, and Oatmeal Soap

Ingredients:
- One bar of a glycerin or castile soap base
- One cup of oatmeal
- One tablespoon of almond oil
- Ten drops of brown sugar and fig fragrance oil

Instructions:
1. Melt the glycerin soap base and combine with the other ingredients.
2. Stir until the mixture has signs of tracing
3. Pour into available molds and cool before cutting.

Herbal Soap Recipes for Antiseptics & Healing

1. Plantain Herbal Soap

Ingredients:

- Two cups of a glycerin soap base
- One handful of plantain leaves or two tablespoons of plantain oil
- One fourth cup of liquid glycerin
- One eighth cup of water

Instructions:

1. Blend the plantain leaves or oil with the liquid glycerin and water. Strain the leaves if preferred.
2. Melt the glycerin soap base and combine with the other ingredients.
3. Stir until the mixture shows signs of tracing.
4. Pour into available molds and cool before cutting.

2. Tea Tree Soap

Ingredients:

- Two cups of a glycerin soap base
- Two tablespoons of tea tree oil

Instructions:

1. Melt the glycerin soap base and combine with the other ingredients.
2. Stir until the soap mixture shows signs of tracing
3. Pour into available molds and cool before cutting.

Other Useful Herbal Soap Recipes

1. **Men's Herbal Shaving Soap**

Ingredients:

- One pound of a glycerin soap base
- One tablespoon of shea butter
- One teaspoon of hemp seed oil
- One teaspoon of olive oil
- A few drops of lemongrass essential oil
- A few drops of clary sage essential oil
- One fourth cup of ground oats

Instructions:

1. Melt the glycerin soap base with a double boiler. Once melted, take the mixture away from the heat and combine with the ground oats.

2. Stir l the soap mixture and add in the base oils and shea butter. The essential oils are added last.

3. Pour into available molds and cool before cutting.

Conclusion

Thank you again for downloading this book!

I hope this book was able to help you to learn the steps to making all natural herbal soaps that keep your skin and body at their best.

The next step is to put the knowledge into action and start living a life enriched by the powerful benefits of homemade herbal soaps.

Finally, if you enjoyed this book, please take the time to share your thoughts and post a review on Amazon. It'd be greatly appreciated!

Thank you and good luck!

Book Description:

Soaps are a regular part of our daily routines. They range from bath soaps, to laundry soaps, to detergents. The obvious function is to help us stay clean in every way. They make us feel fresh and smell nice every day. Despite their popular and wide usage, these soaps can cause many skin related problems and respiratory problems as well. The problem lies in the artificial ingredients used during the manufacturing process. This not only affects us negatively, it also has effects on the environment. While the need for soaps cannot be ignored, the impact that they have on our bodies and on the environment cannot go unnoticed as well.

The solution to the dilemma is to create homemade soaps from scratch. The idea is to use all natural materials that are good for both the body and the environment. There are many other powerful benefits to be gained from this as well.

This book explores the varied concepts and ideas related to homemade soap making combined with natural herb use. Read on and discover the world of herbal soap making and enjoy the unique luxury that they can give. Our lives can be enriched for the better just by taking advantage of nature's little ways of helping us.